EXPLORATIONS

LEWIS AND CLARK AND SACAGAWEA

BY DALTON RAINS

WWW.APEXEDITIONS.COM

Copyright © 2025 by Apex Editions, Mendota Heights, MN 55120. All rights reserved. No part of this book may be reproduced or utilized in any form or by any means without written permission from the publisher.

Apex is distributed by North Star Editions:
sales@northstareditions.com | 888-417-0195

Produced for Apex by Red Line Editorial.

Photographs ©: IanDagnall Computing/Alamy, cover; Shutterstock Images, 1, 6, 7, 8–9, 10–11, 16–17, 18, 19, 21, 25, 26, 27, 29; iStockphoto, 4–5; Bettmann/Getty Images, 12–13; MPI/Archive Photos/Getty Images, 14; American Philosophical Society/Science Source, 22–23; Library of Congress, 24

Library of Congress Control Number: 2024912902

ISBN
979-8-89250-330-3 (hardcover)
979-8-89250-368-6 (paperback)
979-8-89250-441-6 (ebook pdf)
979-8-89250-406-5 (hosted ebook)

Printed in the United States of America
Mankato, MN
012025

NOTE TO PARENTS AND EDUCATORS
Apex books are designed to build literacy skills in striving readers. Exciting, high-interest content attracts and holds readers' attention. The text is carefully leveled to allow students to achieve success quickly. Additional features, such as bolded glossary words for difficult terms, help build comprehension.

CHAPTER 1
THE JOURNEY BEGINS 4

CHAPTER 2
CROSSING THE ROCKIES 10

CHAPTER 3
TO THE COAST AND BACK 16

CHAPTER 4
LASTING IMPACTS 22

COMPREHENSION QUESTIONS • 28
GLOSSARY • 30
TO LEARN MORE • 31
ABOUT THE AUTHOR • 31
INDEX • 32

CHAPTER 1

THE JOURNEY BEGINS

In May 1804, a group of explorers left St. Louis, Missouri. William Clark and Meriwether Lewis led the group. US leaders hired them to explore land west of the Mississippi River.

In 1803, the Louisiana Purchase added land to the United States. US leaders wanted to learn about it.

The explorers built a fort in North Dakota. The Mandan, Hidatsa, and Sahnish peoples lived in this area.

The men took boats along the Missouri River. In late fall, they built a fort near a Hidatsa village. They hired an **interpreter**. His wife, Sacagawea, joined the group, too.

FAR FROM HOME

Sacagawea was Shoshone. But Hidatsa raiders captured and enslaved her. They sold her to a French Canadian **trapper**. Then she was forced to marry him.

Sacagawea (upper left) was about 16 years old when she joined the explorers.

In July 1805, the explorers found the start of the Missouri River.

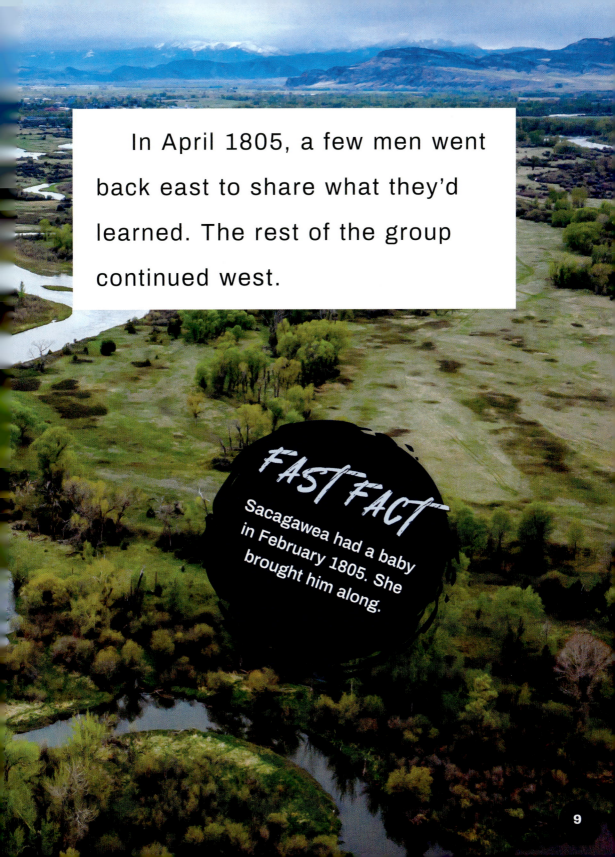

In April 1805, a few men went back east to share what they'd learned. The rest of the group continued west.

FAST FACT
Sacagawea had a baby in February 1805. She brought him along.

CHAPTER 2

CROSSING THE ROCKIES

In August 1805, the group left their boats. They prepared to cross the Rocky Mountains. On the way, they met some Shoshone people. Sacagawea's brother was their leader.

The Rocky Mountains are very tall. Deep snow covers some parts of them.

Sacagawea talked with her brother. He gave the explorers horses. The Shoshone sent a guide with them, too. The weather became very cold. But the group made it across the mountains.

IMPORTANT EXPLORER

Throughout the trip, Sacagawea found plants for people to eat. She made **moccasins** and other clothing. She also helped keep peace and speak with **Indigenous** peoples.

Sacagawea was one of many Indigenous people who helped the explorers.

Next, the explorers made boats from tree trunks. By October, they were floating down the Columbia River.

FAST FACT
If rivers got too rough or shallow, explorers **portaged**. Sometimes they carried their boats for miles.

◀ **The Chinook lived near the Columbia River. They traded with the explorers.**

CHAPTER 3

TO THE COAST AND BACK

In November 1805, the explorers reached the Pacific Ocean. They camped near the coast during winter. In spring, they headed back east.

The explorers built Fort Clatsop and spent their second winter there. This fort is in Oregon.

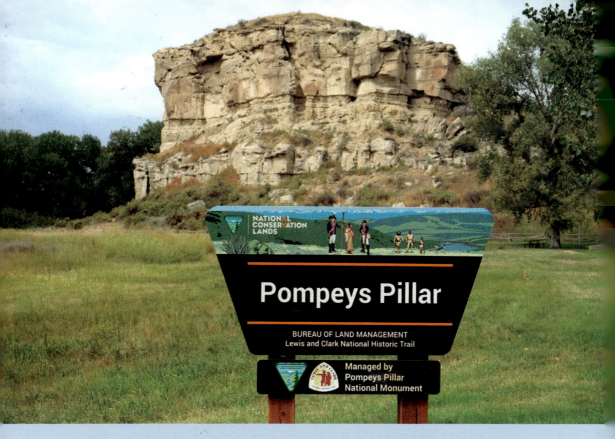

Clark found a large rock. He named it after Sacagawea's son, whose nickname was Pomp.

On July 3, 1806, the group split up. Clark led some men along the Yellowstone River. Sacagawea helped plan their route. Lewis led another group down the Marias River.

DEADLY MEETING

On July 26, Lewis and three explorers met eight Blackfeet people. The two groups camped together. But a fight broke out the next morning. The explorers killed two Blackfeet boys.

Lewis shot a Blackfeet boy who he said was trying to steal.

The groups **reunited** on the Missouri River in August. Sacagawea's family went home. The explorers returned to St. Louis. They arrived in September 1806.

FAST FACT
The explorers traveled nearly 8,000 miles (13,000 km).

Sacagawea didn't get paid for her work. But today, many statues honor her.

CHAPTER 4

LASTING IMPACTS

During the trip, Lewis and Clark kept journals. They wrote about what they did and saw. They made drawings, too. Some were maps. Others showed plants and animals.

Lewis and Clark filled thousands of pages with notes and drawings.

Maps made by Clark were some of the best maps of the West that people had until the 1840s.

US leaders and scientists studied these **documents**. They also studied **samples** the men brought back. They learned about the land and peoples west of the Mississippi River.

FAST FACT
Lewis found 178 plants and 122 animals that scientists hadn't seen before.

Bitterroot was one plant that was new to scientists. Several Indigenous groups used it for food or medicine.

Clark and Sacagawea became friends. He cared for her children after she died in 1812.

Many settlers began moving westward. Indigenous people already lived in the region. But settlers often took their land.

BROKEN PROMISES

Lewis and Clark promised to trade with many Indigenous peoples. US leaders made treaties with peoples, too. But US leaders often broke these agreements.

Today, signs mark the trail Lewis and Clark followed. They help people learn about the expedition.

COMPREHENSION QUESTIONS

Write your answers on a separate piece of paper.

1. Write a few sentences describing how Sacagawea helped the explorers.

2. Would you like to be part of an expedition to map and explore land? Why or why not?

3. When did the explorers reach the Pacific Ocean?
    - A. 1803
    - B. 1805
    - C. 1806

4. How long did the entire journey take?
    - A. less than one year
    - B. about two years
    - C. more than eight years

5. What does **route** mean in this book?

*Clark led some men along the Yellowstone River. Sacagawea helped plan their **route**.*

- **A.** the name of a person
- **B.** the path a group follows
- **C.** the way a fight starts

6. What does **region** mean in this book?

*Many settlers began moving westward. Indigenous people already lived in the **region**. But settlers often took their land.*

- **A.** a type of animal
- **B.** a very large city
- **C.** a part of a country

Answer key on page 32.

GLOSSARY

documents

Papers with written or printed information.

Indigenous

Related to the original people who lived in an area.

interpreter

A person who speaks at least two languages and helps people understand one another.

moccasins

Soft, slip-on shoes, usually made with leather or deerskin.

portaged

Carried a boat over land to reach water.

reunited

Joined back together.

samples

Pieces or examples of things that scientists collect and study.

trapper

A person who catches and sells animals to make money.

treaties

Agreements between two or more countries or groups.

BOOKS

London, Martha. *Sacagawea*. Minneapolis: Abdo Publishing, 2020.

London, Martha. *Thomas Jefferson.* Mendota Heights, MN: Focus Readers, 2023.

Murray, Laura K. *Sacagawea.* North Mankato, MN: Capstone Publishing, 2021.

ONLINE RESOURCES

Visit **www.apexeditions.com** to find links and resources related to this title.

ABOUT THE AUTHOR

Dalton Rains is an author and editor from Saint Paul, Minnesota.

INDEX

B
boats, 6, 10, 15

C
Clark, William, 4, 18, 22, 27

E
explorers, 4, 12, 15, 16, 19–20

H
Hidatsa, 6–7

I
Indigenous peoples, 12, 26–27

J
journals, 22

L
Lewis, Meriwether, 4, 18–19, 22, 25, 27

M
Mississippi River, 4, 24
Missouri River, 6, 20

P
Pacific Ocean, 16

R
Rocky Mountains, 10

S
Sacagawea, 6–7, 9, 10, 12, 18, 20
settlers, 26
Shoshone, 7, 10, 12
St. Louis, Missouri, 4, 20

ANSWER KEY:
1. Answers will vary; 2. Answers will vary; 3. B; 4. B; 5. B; 6. C